Believe and Rediscover Yourself Today!

A 31-Day Journal

Tracy Shorter

Copyright © 2021 Tracy Shorter

ISBN: 978-1-7373670-1-7

All rights reserved.

No part of this publication may be reproduced, distributed, or transmitted in any form or by any means, including photocopying, recording, or other electronic or mechanical methods, without the prior written permission of the publisher, except in the case of brief quotations embodied in critical reviews and certain other noncommercial uses permitted by copyright law.

For individual book orders or author interview requests, visit:

Tracy Shorter Enterprises: www.tracyshorterenterprises.com

Email: tracy@shorterenterprises.net

This Journal Belongs To:

_____

This journal is dedicated to my children, Jasmine and Christian. You have challenged me, pushed me, and supported me. All of this, plus your love, has allowed me to be my BEST. I am grateful and look forward to what the future holds.

Introduction

Ever since I could remember, I have had the desire to help others accomplish their goals -- from assisting my siblings with homework to cooking dinner for my family while my mom worked multiple jobs; even my volunteer activities focused on service to others. Operating in such a manner for a long time put me in a position to not focus on myself, so I became lost for many years.

As I look back over my life's journey, I can remember moments when I wanted to do more towards my self-development. The first time was when I was a stay-at-home mom with a husband and one child. While I loved my daughter and wanted to be everything she needed, just being her mom was not enough to fulfill my inner desires. I knew there had to be more to life. I was just existing, but I was not living. As the years passed by, I had become that person doing life's tasks but not living life to the fullest, mostly because of fear. But fear was not the only thing holding me back. I had to deal with my low self-esteem and peer pressure issues too! I found myself in a hole and had to dig my way out and in doing so, it forced me to re-evaluate who I really was.

In doing so, there were some missteps along the way. For example, I always had the desire to open my own business, so I jumped head-on into being an entrepreneur based on what others said I should be doing. I started business after business, searching for my place, and I received guidance from others instead of truly relying on what did

I want to do and where did God want me to be. And, of course, these quickly failed because my **WHY** was not my own but someone else's.

During my time of rediscovery, I was at a women's ministry event where the minister asked a life-changing question. The question was: What is the one-word God wants me to focus on that year? When I asked myself that question, I did not get an immediate answer. It took a couple of days of meditating on that question for it to become clear. God deposited into my spirit one powerful word, and that is I needed to **BELIEVE**. So, after that, for 12 months, 365 days, I focused on learning what my beliefs were about myself, my business, and my future.

As I began to allow this new word to change my opinion of myself and the possibilities, a new direction began to unfold. It is not new, but my actual purpose became clear. The word **BELIEVE** became seven (7) principles that allowed me to make a transition to a more complete self, thus living my best life.

The principles that unfolded for me were as follows:

B- Be Yourself

E- Empowerment is Key

L- Live Life Now

I- Impossible- Is Possible

E- Encouragement

V- Vision

E- Enjoy Life

So, as you take this journey of self-discovery with me, my desire is that you will apply the principles I found to your own life, that the applications will allow you to not fall into the same pitfalls as I did or if you are already stuck, you can now break free. As you continue this journey we call life, it is true that our beliefs can move our lives in a positive or negative direction. Let's make sure the path you follow brings you positive vibes, peace, and joy. Join me and **BELIEVE** like never before!

Always **BELIEVE** *in Yourself Because I Believe in You.*
-Tracy S.

Day One

The first principle in the **BELIEVE** framework is to **Be Yourself**. We hear that so often, but what does that really mean? To **Be Yourself**, we must understand our identity. Merriam Webster says identity is defined as "the distinguishing character or personality of an individual." In short, it is who you are, the way you think about yourself and are viewed by the world.

In my life, I operated in several roles, including wife, mother, sister, business owner, and community leader, but these titles did not reflect my identity. There were multiple layers woven in between each of these assignments. As I started the journey to being my authentic self, I had to answer honestly some key questions to help me uncover my individual feelings, desires, and characteristics.

Over the next four days, you will do a self-reflection and answer one question each day. These guided questions really gave me some insight into my strengths and weaknesses. Before you answer the questions of the day, please ask God to give you that deep, suppressed answer, the one that you may not even tell your bestie. This is not about those pretty answers you think others want to hear. This is your story, your truth, so be as honest as possible to gain the breakthrough you so well deserve.

Be Yourself

Date_____

What are my values and am I being true to them?

_____
_____
_____
_____
_____
_____
_____
_____
_____
_____
_____
_____
_____
_____
_____
_____
_____
_____
_____
_____
_____

Bonus Action Step(s): Write your core values on a sticky note, the note app in your phone or index cards and view them every day over the next month. This will keep you focused on the values you want others to see in you.

Day Two

There will be times in your life that no matter the amount of planning you do, things just do not go as expected. I remember when my family and I moved into what I felt was our dream home. The place where we, as a couple, would grow old together and play with our grandchildren. It was perfect in my eyes: 4 bedrooms, 3 bathrooms, pool, 2 kids and a dog. We were working consistently to maintain our standard of living and acquire more stuff. The financial promotions at work turned from a blessing to a curse. We lived overextended and that pressure of trying to keep up with other people made us not so appreciative of what we already had.... each other.

When the foreclosure happened, I knew some changes had to take place. The mistakes of the past could not be repeated if we were going to grow old together. As we started over, I was determined to find my happiness and re-connect my family.

Losing that house was the best thing that could have happened for me, for it allowed me the clarity to see that I was displaying my love for my family through material things.

I then decided that our next place would be a home that displayed a thankful heart, respect for each other, and more communication.

Be Yourself

Date_____

Are the people I value the most getting enough of my time? Note below some examples.

_____
_____
_____
_____
_____
_____
_____
_____
_____
_____
_____
_____
_____
_____
_____
_____
_____
_____
_____
_____
_____

Bonus Action Step(s): If your answer to this question was NO, evaluate what is keeping you from spending time with those you genuinely love. If your answer to this question was YES, great job and continue making these memories. Whether YES or No, invite your family or friends to dinner just because and journal about the day.

Day Three

Growing up, my inner circle did not include a lot of people; I was an introvert. Then one day I read a statement by Jim Rohn, that you are the average of the five (5) people you spend the most time with. This was the statement that pushed me to come out of my shell. When you are hurt or afraid of being hurt, it is easier to stay by yourself. But your growth will not occur with that mindset. People are here because we need them, *the right them* that is.

When looking at my circle, there were some that needed to stay and some that needed to go. Hanging out with people who are not happy or always focusing on the negatives of life is shackling. As I was moving out of this shell and expanding my territory with positive influences, my confidence in myself and belief in the possibilities all began to change.

It is important to note that influence did not just mean the people I hung out with on the weekends, but it was the things I chose to read, watch, and the actions taken as well.

Be Yourself

Date_____

What does your Circle of Influence look like? Is it adding or subtracting from your life?

_____
_____
_____
_____
_____
_____
_____
_____
_____
_____
_____
_____
_____
_____
_____
_____
_____
    _____

Bonus Action Step(s): Knowing who to share with and how is important. For those people who are adding to your life, share a kind word of thanks today. If there is anyone subtracting from your life, you may now have to adjust how close they are to you. Be mindful not to share things with those who cannot encourage or give you positive guidance. Negative words do not lead to growth so keep those negative influences at a distance.

Day Four

It is hard to move forward if you are carrying mistakes from your past. It is inevitable that you will make mistakes in life. However, truly forgiving ourselves and others gives us the freedom to see the future without the negative thoughts of the past. This was such a struggle for me until I understood the gift God gave me in forgiveness.

As I said earlier, I was not always a good steward over my finances or family. When I made mistakes in those areas, I would promise or tell myself that I would not repeat them again, but I needed to go further and ask for forgiveness too. It is important to understand what seeking and giving forgiveness provides. It gives you the freedom to move through life without carrying the baggage of past mistakes and regrets. That way when those negative thoughts come, trying to remind you of your past mistakes, you have permission to say it cannot stay.

Use this day to think about those things that keep coming up as unpleasant reminders of your mistakes. Or it could be that there are people in your life you have hurt, and you cannot think of them without getting angry or feeling disappointed. It is time to put in the work to heal any lingering unforgiveness.

Today it is time for you to receive a gift and give one to someone else…the gift we are giving today is the gift of forgiveness.

Be Yourself

Date_____

What unforgiveness or regrets are you carrying in the suitcase called life?

_____
_____
_____
_____
_____
_____
_____
_____
_____
_____
_____
_____
_____
_____
_____
_____
_____
_____
_____
_____
_____

Bonus Action Step(s): Take time and ask for God's forgiveness for the things you have written. Ask Him to help heal your heart from those who have hurt you and give you the ability to forgive them as well.

Day Five

The next letter we will discuss is the **E** in the **BELIEVE** Framework, which means **Empowerment is the Key**! When you think about empowerment, it is the granting of the power, right or authority to perform various acts or duties Merriam Webster's. It is not always easy to empower ourselves; this tends to be easier to do for others. I remember on several occasions giving my empowerment away. It was so easy as I was looking for my peers to believe in me and give me the courage to take the next steps vs. believing in myself regardless of outside opinions. Seeking advice or suggestions from those you trust is not giving away your empowerment because we indeed need that special community of people.

I remember when I decided to discontinue the decor services offered by my event planning company. When looking at the opportunity for profits, it was true that this division helped our profit line tremendously. But the more I operated out of alignment just based on my profit margin, the unhappier I became. I know this is probably not a popular statement and there were indeed other options such as outsourcing the projects or hiring someone else to manage the division, but even with these options, the success would still require my input, and I was not ready to continue down that path. So, regardless of the thoughts of others, I empowered myself to make the decision that was going to make me happy, even when others did not understand my why.

Empowerment is the Key

Date_____

Have you ever thought about empowering yourself? What area in your life could benefit from that inward reflection?

_____
_____
_____
_____
_____
_____
_____
_____
_____
_____
_____
_____
_____
_____
_____
_____
_____
_____
_____
_____

Bonus Action Step(s): Offer some empowering words to someone in your circle this week.

Day Six

Life is too short to continue sitting on the sidelines dreaming. This is exactly what I did every time we went to the beach because I didn't know how to swim. To mask my inability, I started telling myself that the beach wasn't enjoyable, and the mountains were my favorite place to be.

It was a trip to Destin, FL with my family where I really examined my issues with swimming. My husband and kids decided they wanted to rent a Sea-doo Jet Ski. As they were getting ready to go, everyone started handing me all the items they wanted me to hold on to until they returned. As I walked up and down the boardwalk window shopping, I realized I was totally alone, and I did not like the feeling of being left behind. It was not until I got honest with myself and acknowledged that I really wanted to be in the water, but fear was keeping me on dry land. There are plenty of excuses we tell ourselves to keep from trying something new in life. We use age and of course the old saying, "You can't teach an old dog new tricks." I say yes you can, it just requires more patience.

It was on this trip that I decided I was going to learn how to swim because the next time we rented Sea-doos, it was going to be as a family unit, so I am taking the first step with learning how to swim.

Empowerment is the Key

Date_____

Name one (1) new thing you would like to learn to do and why.

_____
_____
_____
_____
_____
_____
_____
_____
_____
_____
_____
_____
_____
_____
_____
_____
_____
_____
_____
_____

Bonus Action Step(s): Determine the first step you need to do to learn the thing you journaled above. Give yourself a deadline to start this new activity.

Day Seven

During Day Six, I shared with you how my fear kept me from learning to swim. I was not just operating in fear but also its cousin called Doubt. I am sure you are not like this, but the way my brain works, I must be knowledgeable before I start new projects. For things I'm not well versed in, I would first need to gather all the information and oftentimes, this overload made me lack my abilities even more.

I now understand that sometimes taking the first step to JUMP is more important than reading up on how to JUMP. It is likely there is more than one thing keeping you from living life to the fullest or playing full out, but today we are going to focus on that number one thought that keeps coming up when you think about starting something new in your life.

A friend of mine spoke on a scripture in Philippians 4:8 (KJV) that says "Finally, brethren, whatsoever things are true, whatsoever things are honest, whatsoever things are just, whatsoever things are pure, whatsoever things are lovely, whatsoever things are of good report; if there be any virtue, and if there be any praise, think on these things."

Learning to use this scripture in my life was a game-changer. The fear I had put up on a mantle was not true; it was not pure, lovely, or of a good report. Therefore, I did not need to give it the attention it was getting; instead, I needed to continue stepping forward. In doing so my faith and confidence within myself increased and my abilities too.

Empowerment is the Key

Date_____

Write below what is the number one (1) obstacle standing in the way of your happiness.

_____
_____
_____
_____
_____
_____
_____
_____
_____
_____
_____
_____
_____
_____
_____
_____
_____

Bonus Action Step(s): Partner with someone to do something out of character. Experience something new.

Day Eight

I am sure you have heard the saying that the glass is either half full or half empty. The answer is based on how the person views what they see. Over the years, as I was looking at my glass, my focus was based on what was *missing* from the glass. I forgot to be thankful for the fact I had a glass at all to fill.

This can be an easy trap to fall into, yet a dangerous one as well because it can lead to heartache. The blessing is not just what is in the glass but that it's **your glass**. Like the people in our lives, taking them for granted is just like not appreciating the glass.

I spent a great deal of my time working and volunteering with the hope that the result would be that I was able to completely fill my glass. What happened instead is I left some of the people I cared about deeply feeling neglected. I write this to remind you to look at the end goal and examine what you desire your life to be and then work your way back to the middle.

The things I was pushing for and thought were most important were not as important to the people I loved. So, remember to be thankful for the glass, the liquid inside, and the fact that you have room to fill or even overflow your glass.

Empowerment is the Key

Date_____

At the end of the day, what do you want your life to be about? Share your thoughts on the topic of appreciating the glass half full.

_____
_____
_____
_____
_____
_____
_____
_____
_____
_____
_____
_____
_____
_____
_____
_____
_____
_____
_____
_____

Bonus Action Step(s): When faced with stressful situations, work hard to find the positive aspect. Remember the glass half full concept.

Day Nine

The **L** in **BELIEVE** tells us to **Live Life Now**. So often we put off until tomorrow the things we can do today. The issue with this is we do not know what tomorrow could look like and it is not even promised to us. I heard a quote by an Unknown Author that said, "The saddest summary of life contains three descriptions: could have, might have, and should have." So what does the statement **Live Life Now** really mean?

It is taking the opportunity today to tell people you care about how much they mean to you; it is taking the time to help others, and it is taking the time to care for yourself and do those things that will make each day better than the last. The long and short of it is it's about living a life with no regrets!

It was a Wednesday afternoon in October when I received a call from my doctor that scared me so badly, I had to look at my life. It was not so much the diagnosis as it was the fear of losing the life I had become accustomed to and even the one I was building. But then I realized I had to make the most of every opportunity. I had to get into the game and live the life I was meant to -- not tomorrow, but today.

Let's take the next few days and examine some areas that may help you refocus and recommit to living your best life now.

Live Life Now

Date_____

What can you do today to make life better for yourself or someone else?

_____
_____
_____
_____
_____
_____
_____
_____
_____
_____
_____
_____
_____
_____
_____
_____
_____
_____
_____
_____

Bonus Action Step(s): Call a friend and check on them today.

Day Ten

To make the journey towards living my best life, there were at least two areas that needed an immediate change. The first one was MY FINANCES. Everyone would agree money is required to live life to the fullest, but I mismanaged the resources I was blessed with to say the least. Instead of just talking about a budget, I sat down and created one.

But I had already gotten over my head in debt. I realized all too quickly I was spending too much, eating out and buying clothes. The house, car notes, credit card debt, student loans, kids' activities, plus other monthly housing expenses meant some drastic cuts had to happen. Now it took me a minute to accept that my largest expense, my house, had to go.

I clearly remember sitting in the middle of the bed looking at papers from my mortgage company and having a somber reality check. I could either continue making the bank account-breaking payment or give my dream house back. I chose the latter. One of the biggest mistakes was purchasing a house based on the top level of our income bracket. You need to leave room for life's unexpected changes. On our final day at that house, I was not sure if life was ever going to be good again. However, I learned it was not the house that made the home; it's the people in it. As we began to rebuild with financial responsibility, I soon realized I was the happiest I had ever been.

Live Life Now

Date_____

Do you need to make any improvements on how to handle finances so you can live more freely? If so, what?

_____

_____

_____

_____

_____

_____

_____

_____

_____

_____

_____

_____

_____

_____

_____

_____

_____

_____

_____

Bonus Action Step(s): If you do not have a budget or app for your finances, consider using one. If you already have a budget, review and be sure that it still works for your family's needs.

Day Eleven

Yesterday, I shared with you one thing in my life that needed an immediate change; today I will share the second. The second thing was MY HEALTH. For years, I was eating whatever I desired and most of it could be called stress eating. I used food to compensate for lack of funds, the increased debt and low self-esteem. I thought that my height would hide the increased pounds, but it did not, and it only got harder to move around.

I cannot say that weight was the only issue when it came to my health. My heartbeat was extremely irregular, which made it difficult for me to keep a solid exercise routine. An examination led to be being diagnosed with a Pseudo Tumor Celibri. A Pseudo Tumor Celibri is a condition where pressure inside the skull increases for no obvious reason. The symptoms mimic a brain tumor, but no tumor is present. Persons with this diagnosis can experience severe headaches, blurred vision, ringing in the ears in time with your heartbeat or brief episodes of blindness. All of this within a three-year period made me really say **enough is enough.**

Losing weight has been an up and down journey because the approach I was taking gave me quick but temporary results. It was then I committed to just a total lifestyle change regarding food and exercise. I still enjoy my favorite dishes and desserts, but I do allow them to be consumed in moderation. It's ok to enjoy the pleasures of life, but we must have discipline as well.

Live Life Now

Date_____

Ask yourself: Am I being my healthy self? If not, what areas need improvement?

_____
_____
_____
_____
_____
_____
_____
_____
_____
_____
_____
_____
_____
_____
_____
_____
_____
_____
_____
_____

Bonus Action Step(s): Record all the food and beverages you eat for one (1) week using apps like My Fitness Pal. This will allow you to see if you are eating too many calories, getting enough water, and exercising. If you need to improve in one area, just tackle them one at a time and commit to the change for the rest of the month.

Day Twelve

When it comes to my current career, for many years, I never viewed it as a career. It was just a job. When my husband and I got married, I worked outside the home until we were expecting our second child, Christian. After Christian was born, we made the decision that I would stay home until the kids were school age. That was a decision that had so many unexpected feelings for me, and I could not wait to get back into the workforce.

When I decided to go back to work, there was no strategy, it was just **get a job**. The non-negotiable requirement was I needed to be home on nights and weekends. As I filled out my paperwork at the temporary agency, I had no clue what I wanted or could do. The job I ended up with is still the job I am doing today as an Associate in Public Finance, and that was twenty-three years ago as of this writing.

As I reflect on my current position, I realized that God opened a door for me, but I had not always taken full advantage of the possibilities. My primary thought was to help provide for my family, not how the job was fulfilling for me. But now, I view things differently. The thoughts of age, time, and experience play a big part with my thought process. However, it's never too late to operate in your purpose. God can restore the time.

Live Life Now

Date_____

Do you love your current career or is it time for a change?

_____
_____
_____
_____
_____
_____
_____
_____
_____
_____
_____
_____
_____
_____
_____
_____
_____
_____
_____
_____

Bonus Action Step(s): If you have found the perfect career, congratulations! If not, it's time to create a strategy that will position you to do what you love vs. just doing a job.

Day Thirteen

Today we start the letter **I** in **BELIEVE**, which means Impossible, but we are going to focus on what Is Possible. Thinking that things are impossible happens when we focus only on what we see and stop working towards what could be. As a teenager, I saw many places I wanted to visit in books and movies, but never really believed I would visit these places.

However, for my 40th milestone birthday, I got the opportunity to go to Paris and London. Seeing the Eiffel Tower and Buckingham Palace in person was life-changing. It is not that these places had such significant importance to me, but they were landmarks I wondered about and never thought I would get to see in person until much later in life. The things in life we desire to experience can come in many ways. If it is a dream vacation, it can be through planning and saving your funds over time. Opening the doors to what you think is impossible could even come from your network of people.

What's most important to remember is not how you receive the opportunity but to believe that the opportunities are available to you too. It's time to remove the thoughts of impossibilities from your life and focus on how to make them possibilities.

Impossible – Is possible

Date_____

List things you have viewed as impossibilities. Follow up with the bonus step below.

_____
_____
_____
_____
_____
_____
_____
_____
_____
_____
_____
_____
_____
_____
_____
_____
_____
_____
_____
_____
_____
_____

Bonus Action Step(s): Do research or make a checklist of things that need to happen to accomplish one thing you listed above.

Impossible – Is possible

Day Fourteen

Yesterday, I shared with you the start of my mind shift regarding possibilities. When I look back, the actions we take are important but another ingredient to my mind shift was learning to be more open-minded. Being open-minded doesn't mean you agree with everyone, but it does mean that you are willing to listen more and sometimes talk less. My two children can be referred to as a Ying and Yang pair. They often share the same opinion on a topic, but their approaches are entirely different.

As the parent, I felt I should be doing the teaching; I had not considered that they could teach me something new as well. I felt it was my job to provide instructions for them to follow. But these little people we call children grow to have personalities and sometimes differing opinions from ours. Much of this is based on experiences they encounter on their journey of discovery. It wasn't until I was having a conversation with my daughter about church. She was being respectful, but I wasn't really listening. After allowing some time to pass and a conversation with a trusted confidant, I realized I was closed-minded. Not only was it closed but I lacked knowledge of many topics impacting the world and my children because I was too busy talking and not doing enough listening.

After a while, I approached the subject again. It was one of the most thought-provoking conversations we've shared as a child and parent. Now, I didn't agree with every point of view she shared, but I did receive insight that has allowed me to communicate better with not just her but with people.

Impossible – Is possible

Date_____

In what area do you lack knowledge that will improve your life?

_____
_____
_____
_____
_____
_____
_____
_____
_____
_____
_____
_____
_____
_____
_____
_____
_____
_____
_____
_____
_____

Bonus Action Step(s): Do a Google search to enlighten yourself about the area you listed above. Explore the possibilities.

Day Fifteen

Our actions are driven by our thoughts. This is true and determines what we get accomplished. Mindset is defined by Merriam Webster as a "habitual or characteristic mental attitude that determines how you will interpret and respond to situations." I knew this but putting it into practice in my personal life proved to be more challenging than in my business life.

In addition to my day job, I also serve as a travel agent-more on that later. When I'm servicing clients for travel, especially my wedding couples, no matter what challenges we faced, I never gave up. Believe me, there were many challenges along the way, but giving up was not an option.

Clients have lost their dream location due to an act of God; some have dealt with unreliable vendors who did not deliver the product; there were even a few wardrobe disasters. I had such a heart to see the people I served WIN and when obstacles arose, I went into problem-solving mode. However, when it came to my personal challenges, I tended to have a lot of excuses as to why it could not work.

I soon realized my mindset had expectations that others were more deserving or capable, so that is why I worked harder for them than myself. My mindset had to shift; the same energy I gave to others I now needed to give permission for that to operate in my life as well. I am not sure who said it, but I remember being told that as quickly as the limiting belief came, it could leave just as quickly based on the word or deed I did next. In other words, my impossible became possible. This was not a quick process by any means, but over time I found myself contradicting my negative by looking for solutions.

Impossible – Is possible

Date_____

List the dreams and desires you have for yourself.

_____
_____
_____
_____
_____
_____
_____
_____
_____
_____
_____
_____
_____
_____
_____
_____
_____
_____
_____
_____
_____
_____
_____
_____
_____
_____
_____

Bonus Action Step(s): Based on your list above, work on at least one.

Impossible – Is possible

Day Sixteen

We have spent the last couple of reflections talking about how the things we view as impossible can become possibilities in our life. To close out this chapter, I want you to remember the following words:

The **IMPOSSIBLE** is only possible when I understand the difference between **I CAN** and **I DON'T WANT TOO**.

Think about the *Watty Piper children's story "The Little Engine Who Could."* That little caboose presented with a challenge was totally willing to accept the job, even though he didn't see himself as strong as the other train cars. Let's think for a minute: What if he was asked to pull the cars up the track and he didn't want to do the job in the first place?

The task would have been even harder because of his attitude, and it's likely he would not have achieved the success he did. Wanting to participate in something is half the battle to getting the successful result desired. If you have those tasks in your life that feel or seem to be impossible for you to reach, ask yourself this question first: Is this something I really want to do?

Be your own little engine. If it's something you want to do but haven't taken that first leap, do it today. Take the first step and say...I think I can, I think I can and guess what? YOU CAN!

Impossible – Is possible

Date_____

What are some areas in your life where you could use an attitude adjustment? List them below.

_____
_____
_____
_____
_____
_____
_____
_____
_____
_____
_____
_____
_____
_____
_____
_____
_____
_____
_____
_____
_____

Bonus Action Step(s): Be bold and ask a friend about what areas you could improve upon?

Day Seventeen

Today we will start the next E, which is **ENCOURAGEMENT**. There will be times in life when a curve ball happens, and you will not have anyone to tell you that it's going to be all right. It is in these times that you will need the right words to keep you going. It's great having a support system, but they cannot be with you 24-hours a day to keep you pumped up. Besides, the words that come out of your mouth have more power over the direction of your life.

When the medical challenges in my life happened, my support system was a source of strength. But when it's 3 am in the morning and you are in pain, you don't always feel right calling someone. It was in these moments I had to learn how to encourage myself. What I decided to do was write down words of affirmation in places I could see them daily. I used sticky notes and wrote down words I wanted to embrace, but I was not fully there yet BELIEVING them to be true.

Every day, I would read these affirmations and as time went on, I was hearing them in my dreams. It was then that I knew some changes were taking place. I was not just speaking words of power; I was believing there was **power in the words**. As my belief increased, so did my healing process. I learned that the work I did to encourage my mentality was just as important as my physical work to aid in my healing.

Encouragement

Date_____

Do you have a daily encouragement routine? If so, what is it? If not, how can you encourage yourself daily?

_____
_____
_____
_____
_____
_____
_____
_____
_____
_____
_____
_____
_____
_____
_____
_____
_____
_____
_____
_____
_____

Bonus Action Step(s): Use sticky notes and write 3-5 affirmations that you will recite daily. Post these in a place where you can see them, repeating them at least 3 times a day. Assess how you feel at the end of a week.

Encouragement

Day Eighteen

I was preparing for work when my friend Yakinea Marie came on Facebook Live with one of her 6 AM inspiration sessions. I was listening and dressing, but my ears really got in tune when she asked us to write an I AM statement. I had never done this, and it was a little challenging. I started searching for adjectives I thought applied and then saw this statement by Gary Hensel that states:

I AM.........

two of the most powerful words, for what you put after them shapes your reality.

So, with that, I started writing words I desired for my life as well as those that already applied. I was then able to get my forty (40) I AM statements quickly.

Encouragement

Date_____

What do you believe about yourself? Fill in a word behind I AM below that describes yourself.

1. I AM_____

2. I AM_____

3. I AM_____

4. I AM_____

5. I AM_____

6. I AM_____

7. I AM_____

8. I AM_____

9. I AM_____

10. I AM_____

Encouragement

11. I AM _____

12. I AM _____

13. I AM _____

14. I AM _____

15. I AM _____

16. I AM _____

17. I AM _____

18. I AM _____

19. I AM _____

20. I AM _____

Bonus Action Step(s): Add 20 more I AM statements and post them where you can see them daily.

Encouragement

Encouragement

Day Nineteen

Growing up, there was a saying: "Sticks and stones will break my bones, but words will never harm me." This is true; words do not have the tendency to create physical harm, but mentally, the wrong words can do great damage. As a very tall, awkward girl growing up, I lacked self-esteem and belief in myself. I used to believe that old saying about words not harming me. I did not understand the power they had in reverse.

When I did the I AM assignment in the previous chapter, it was a revelation for me. The way I felt repeating all those statements about myself is the way I wanted to feel every day. For that to happen, I had to change my environment. You may wonder what exactly does that mean? It means removing myself from negative influences or forces. Replacing the negative energy with positive influences, like listening to people who spoke or had accomplished what I desired. But most important, changing the words I spoke out of my mouth about myself.

What comes out of your mouth is what you hear; what you hear can be what you believe, thus what you believe is what you will receive. Speak life and not death to yourself, your family, and those around you. Then watch how more positive things begin to manifest in your life.

Encouragement

Date_____

Think back. Do you tend to speak more negative or positive statements in life? Note your reflection below.

_____
_____
_____
_____
_____
_____
_____
_____
_____
_____
_____
_____
_____
_____
_____
_____
_____
_____
_____
_____
_____

Bonus Action Step(s): In order to be blessed, sow some positive seeds into someone else's life.

Encouragement

Day Twenty

The last couple of days, we've had discussions about how to speak positive thoughts about yourself, but what about others? I am going to be very transparent today. I thought I was always a person who sincerely celebrated the accomplishments of others, but that was not true.

I realized I had jealousy tendencies. I say this because I saw people around me accomplishing things in their business and personal lives that I was working so hard to get as well. I was confused why they were moving fast, and it seemed I was still crawling.

At this point in my life, I was really working on my personal relationship with God and prayer life. I can tell you if you ask God a question and you honestly are open to hearing the answer, you will receive one. That was the case with me in this area. It was revealed to me that I was secretly operating with a *crab in a barrel* mentality.

However, as a crab in the barrel, my purpose was not to continue climbing over the other crabs but to help them to see that if we worked together, we could all get out of the barrel. This meant truly being happy, cheering, and assisting others with the gift that God had placed in my life --the gift to help others birth and grow their purpose. Even if those I helped looked to be exceeding my own goals, it was ok. The reason it was ok was because my elevation in this season is not just tied to my hard work but my obedience to the call on my life. The call to help others **BELIEVE** in themselves, be a support to them, and push them to the finish line.

Encouragement

Date_____

Are you a supporter of others or do you need to improve in this area? Note your reflection below.

_____
_____
_____
_____
_____
_____
_____
_____
_____
_____
_____
_____
_____
_____
_____
_____
_____
_____
_____
_____
_____
_____

Bonus Action Step(s): Support a small local business owner.

Vision

Day Twenty-One

Today we will start our next letter, the **V** for **VISION**. Whether you have a life or business vision you are working towards, there will be times of disappointments or setbacks. It is during this moment you must rely on your WHY. Understanding what ignites you can keep the flame from burning out completely. Knowing this will serve as a source of motivation when things are not going well so that you do not give up.

When I first started my event planning company, it was because people said that it was something I could do to make me some money. While this is usually the first motivation for many businesses, it will not keep you in business. I realized that helping others achieve their vision was something I was deeply passionate about, and it made me want to get out of bed each day. When clients had problems paying for services, I still wanted to help. Now I am not saying you should not be compensated well for your services; you should. But there will be days when the money will not generate as you hoped. If you are dedicated to your vision, it is something you will still want to see through. For me, it was a YES!

In life, you will have dreams and things that you want to see realized. Knowing why you want to achieve these goals will help you stay on course.

Vision

Date_____

What is your WHY statement?

_____
_____
_____
_____
_____
_____
_____
_____
_____
_____
_____
_____
_____
_____
_____
_____
_____
_____
_____
_____
_____
_____
_____
_____
_____
_____

Bonus Action Step(s): Think of one thing that makes you happy and do it with someone today.

Vision

Day Twenty-Two

I have always been a VISIONARY, but I have not always had a written Vision or understood its importance. In **Habakkuk 2:2** KJV states *"Write the vision, and make it plain upon tables, that he may run that readeth it."* Vision is defined by the Oxford dictionary as "the ability to think about or plan the future with imagination or wisdom." To most people, this could be called dreaming -- thinking and hoping for things that have not come to pass just yet. But there is a key word in the definition above that needs to be remembered: it's the word PLAN.

To create a plan requires you to have steps of action. A written plan is even more productive because it allows you to see where you are, what needs to happen next, and the final picture. Besides, I believe that plans that are written tend to get accomplished more than those that stay in your head.

For years, I followed this process in my business as an Event Planner and not my personal life. But creating a written vision is not just a business practice. Once I started thinking about the vision for my business and personal life and how they were connected, I knew having a written plan for both was going to allow me to accomplish more. Thus, the process started with quarterly goals that were evaluated at the end of each quarter. My goals are now not two separate plans, but a comprehensive one that merges my business and personal life.

Vision

Date_____

Write three (3) goals you would like to accomplish in the next 90 days.

_____
_____
_____
_____
_____
_____
_____
_____
_____
_____
_____
_____
_____
_____
_____
_____
_____
_____
_____
_____
_____
_____
_____
_____
_____

Bonus Action Step(s): Write a plan for how you will accomplish one of the goals.

Vision

Day Twenty-Three

Writing my goals was just the first step to getting them accomplished. The most important asset I had was not money or people but time. I had to do a better job of managing this valuable resource. Today, I will share some time management tips to help you make the most of your day.

- Use a planner, which can be either physical or digital, but it needs to show both monthly and weekly features.

- Use the planner to block out times for all your different activities (i.e., social media, gym, client call, personal time, etc.)

- If it's not on the calendar, then you should not be doing it. There will be times when you will receive those unexpected phone calls from family or friends asking you to join them for dinner or coffee. These are important activities but should be scheduled during the personal time blocks on your calendar.

- Scheduling your day is vital to getting things accomplished. Be sure to make a to-do list at the end of each day for the next day.

- Sometimes you will have to just say NO! Learn what you can do and what is too much for your schedule.

Vision

Date_____

Write out your to-do list for today.

Bonus Action Step(s): Stick to your to-do list today and continue this exercise for the next week.

Day Twenty-Four

As we dig a little deeper into accomplishing our goals, understand you cannot do this alone. The most successful people have a great team and network around them. This was a little challenging for me, as I consider myself an introvert. I am totally open to helping others when needed. However, networking to meet new people was something I avoided because I didn't talk very much.

When I started Tracy Shorter Events, I did not fully think out how I was going to execute the final product for my clients without help. Like many small business owners, my company was not in the position to hire paid staffing at the beginning. Without the support of family and friends, I could not have produced the result needed to get continued referrals. I say this as a reminder to value the people in your life.

Networking with others is not only about getting something from someone but can be a great opportunity for you to give to others as well. Just as you are looking for your missing puzzle pieces, you are the missing puzzle piece to someone else. We can all experience the beauty a complete picture offers when we work together.

Vision

Date_____

List some people you would like to connect with personally or for your business.

_____
_____
_____
_____
_____
_____
_____
_____
_____
_____
_____
_____
_____
_____
_____
_____
_____
_____
_____
_____
_____
_____
_____
_____

Bonus Action Step(s): Plan to reach out to two (2) of the people you listed above.

Day Twenty-Five

We are almost at the end of our journey, and we have one more letter to tackle and that is the last **E** for **Enjoy Life** which is a vital part of the journey. But what does that really mean? For each person, it's going to be different. After years of being on the hamster wheel, taking care of others before myself, I had finally learned to add myself to the calendar. Having a self-care plan helps you to reset; it gives you an understanding of who you are and who you are not. This happens because your focus shifts from others to yourself...hence the words SELF CARE PLAN.

I remember the first time I treated myself to a spa treatment. Looking at the menu of services and the prices, I was thinking there is no way I can spend this much on just one thing, especially when the kids still needed things too. But I had committed to giving myself that experience and had saved for it, so I just kept battling with my little voice. Sitting in the quiet spa room waiting, I was still focused on the cost, then the massage tech called my name for my service. As I walked into the very dimly lit room, I had to admit it was a relaxing atmosphere. As the tech started the treatment, the thoughts about how much this was costing just drifted away.

As she finished up the massage, I realized it was well worth the money. It was the best experience of my life and something I wanted to incorporate quarterly but at a minimum twice a year.

To be the best for everyone else you must first be the best YOU for yourself.

Enjoy Life

Date_____

Do you have a self-care plan and what does it include? If you don't have a plan create one.

_____
_____
_____
_____
_____
_____
_____
_____
_____
_____
_____
_____
_____
_____
_____
_____
_____
_____
_____
_____

Bonus Action Step(s): Make plans to put into action this week one of your self-care tips.

Enjoy Life

Day Twenty-Six

Planning events had become my passion and the idea of merging that passion and travel was a dream come true. So, when the opportunity came to add travel planning as a service, I jumped at the chance to become a travel agent. Becoming a travel agent would allow me the opportunity to see the world and help others do the same. I started thinking about what location was going to give me my first passport stamp. The location that won out was Jamaica.

After the trip to Jamaica, I decided to create a personal bucket list of experiences and locations I was going to visit. My list was not just domestic locations but included some international ones as well. I began the planning, one location at a time, with the hope of creating memories that would last me a lifetime. It may seem like a simple thing -- creating a list, but writing it down made me want to be more accountable to the list.

So far, I have been able to see four locations on my list -- two which were mentioned earlier (Paris and London.) I have also been to Spain and part of France. Based on my current plan, the other locations will be marked off my list within the next three years. The great part about all this is it's just not something for me, but something my family can experience too. It's time to create your own bucket list too.

Enjoy Life

Date_____

Create your personal bucket list of travel locations and/or experiences.

_____
_____
_____
_____
_____
_____
_____
_____
_____
_____
_____
_____
_____
_____
_____
_____
_____
_____
_____
_____
_____
_____
_____

Bonus Action Step(s): Is there one experience on your bucket list that you can experience this week? If so, create the plan and journal about it.

Enjoy Life

Day Twenty-Seven

One task that is important to master in the enjoyment of life and all it has to offer is learning to be grateful. Things are not going to always go as planned and it's in these moments that having a sense of gratefulness is vital. I heard my pastor once say sometimes it seems that those who are successful just get more successful and those who appear unsuccessful continue to get more unsuccessful. When I heard those words, I knew that I had experienced the same thoughts, but then the question of WHY rose to my mind.

I knew in the race to achieve what I perceived as success, I was not a very grateful person for what had already been accomplished. It's not that we are to not strive for more and challenge ourselves to do better. But every day we wake up, there is an opportunity for another chance and choice. As Nina Simone's song *Feeling Good* says, "It's a new day, It's a new dawn, It's a new life…for me." Thru my gratitude box, which is a small wooden with index cards that I write on each day I started to have a greater appreciation for life. This allowed me to count my blessing for the small things and be in praise mode for the things to come.

Enjoy Life

Date_____

What in life are you grateful for today?

_____
_____
_____
_____
_____
_____
_____
_____
_____
_____
_____
_____
_____
_____
_____
_____
_____
_____
_____
_____
_____
_____
_____

Bonus Action Step(s): Write down something you are grateful for at the end of each day for the next week.

Day Twenty-Eight

Realizing how much I must be grateful for, it became apparent that I also needed to sow some joy into the lives of others. It's natural to do this with people we hold close, like family and friends. But what about people you don't know? The impact of creating a smile on their faces or supplying a need can create a domino effect in the lives of others.

I remember one Monday morning pulling into the McDonald's parking lot with only $20, which needed to last the entire week. However, I really wanted a caramel Frappuccino and Sausage Egg and Cheese McGriddle, so I ordered one. As I pulled to the cashier's window, I was informed that my order had been upgraded and paid in full. I was getting the medium drink instead of the small I originally ordered. The car ahead of me had purchased my breakfast and didn't wait to give me the opportunity to say thank you. Instead, they left me with a card that read "GOD LOVES YOU."

Looking at that card just made my day and reminded me that everything was going to be all right. From this experience, I learned that even the smallest of deeds can make a difference. Now, I needed to randomly pay forward the act of kindness given to me so many years ago.

Self-Reflection

Date_____

What small act of kindness can you do that will allow someone else to have a great day?

_____
_____
_____
_____
_____
_____
_____
_____
_____
_____
_____
_____
_____
_____
_____
_____
_____
_____
_____
_____
_____

Bonus Action Step(s): Perform your act of kindness randomly this week.

Self-Reflection

Day Twenty-Nine

Use this space to meditate on which chapters spoke most to you and why.

Self-Reflection

Self-Reflection

Day Thirty

Use this day to sit in a quiet space for 15 minutes meditating on the work you've done using this journal; note below what you're feeling and if there are action steps, start doing something today!

_____
_____
_____
_____
_____
_____
_____
_____
_____
_____
_____
_____
_____
_____
_____

Self-Reflection

Self-Reflection

Day Thirty-One

Use this space to list all those who would benefit from using this journal and why. Then start sharing the good news.

Self-Reflection

My Prayer for You

My prayer is that the roadblocks in your life are now open pathways that will allow you to get off the sidelines and enter the starting line of **LIFE**. May you be **BOLD** in your words and next steps. May you now see the word **BELIEVE** and always remember to apply the principles it represents to your life. May relationships be renewed; may you create lifetime memories with family and friends and be open to travel the different avenues of life so your eyes can be opened to the beauty this world has to offer. Know that today can be the beginning of the best days of your life. All you must do now is **BELIEVE**. Amen.

Always Believe in Yourself.

Your Cheerleader for Life,

Tracy

Acknowledgments and Special Thanks to the Following People:

Rolando Shorter, you have supported this new journey of my life and I am blessed beyond measure to have you as my partner. The successes are easier because of your support and encouragement.

Makeda Dabney, while I am cheering for others you have always cheered for me!

Pastor(s) Larry and Tracy Russell, the words you have spoken into my life made a difference. Thanks for believing in me.

About Tracy Shorter

Whenever you interact with Tracy Shorter, one thing for sure is going to happen. You will leave encouraged, supported, and have a new cheerleader on this journey we call LIFE! With a strong servant's heart and over fourteen years of strategic planning experience, she has been helping women fulfill their vision and create memories through planning weddings, live events, and travel under Tracy Shorter Enterprises. Then in 2016, the Lord spoke the word **BELIEVE** to Tracy. Unbeknownst to her, she would need it more than ever in 2018, when an unexpected health forecast came without warning. After months of prayer, the message was clear: Simply **BELIEVE!** It was not just a direct word to Tracy, but she was to spread that message to other women around her and a new purpose unfolded to help women live life to its full potential.

Reach out to Tracy:

Tracy Shorter Enterprises: www.shorterenterprises.com

Email: tracy@shorterenterprises.net

www.ingramcontent.com/pod-product-compliance
Lightning Source LLC
Chambersburg PA
CBHW062151100526
44589CB00014B/1783